Teaching Mindfulness To Teenage Students

Faye Carlisle

Table of Contents

Introduction

You may have heard about the benefits of mindfulness but not been sure how to implement it in your school. This practical guide explains how to teach mindfulness to groups of students in a school setting. It outlines lesson plans for teaching mindfulness over twelve sessions with links to free downloadable PowerPoints for the busy teacher.

What is mindfulness?

Mindfulness involves paying attention to the present moment and becoming more aware of thoughts and feelings. It also involves being able to let go of thoughts and feelings that cause us anxiety.

For example, a teacher may spend too much time worrying about a conversation they had with pupil last week or worrying about a promotion. They may get themselves so worked up about dealing with the behaviour of a certain class that they forget how to make learning fun. The people who experience the least stress at work are often the people who just focus on the tasks at hand rather than spending their time worrying about other things. Mindfulness training helps people to be more effective at work as well as reducing stress.

A teenager may come into a lesson and be unable

to concentrate because his thoughts are preoccupied with an argument he has had with a girlfriend. He starts ruminating on the argument and imagining that his girlfriend's parents will never talk to him again. We can all add to our problems if we let ourselves but it isn't particularly constructive. Practising mindfulness can reduce our tendency to do this.

Schools offer the ideal setting to help teenagers learn the skills necessary to deal with their relationships and other stressors in their lives. Short mindfulness based sessions can be timetabled into the school day. Tutors in schools often do not know the best way to fill their tutorial time but mindfulness is one thing that can easily be carried out by everyone.

However, a word of caution: Before mindfulness can be taught, students and the teachers themselves need to be persuaded that it is effective. If students are unwilling to participate or if teachers are cynical about its effectiveness, then it won't work.

So how do you convince people in a school that mindfulness works?

People are usually persuaded by hard evidence and there is a lot of scientific research to support mindfulness. I've found that the showing teachers and students brain scans of how the brain actually changes after practising mindfulness is particularly convincing.

So the first thing that you need to do is show teachers and students a presentation on the research evidence for the effectiveness of mindfulness.

Research Evidence

Holzel and colleagues (2011) looked at the effect on a group of people of taking part in an eight week Mindfulness Based Stress Reduction programme. They carried out brain scans on the participants who were spending about half an hour a day practising mindfulness. They found that the participants had increased grey matter in parts of the brain related to self-awareness, compassion and self-reflection. They also found decreased grey matter in the amygdala, a region of the brain related to feelings of anxiety and aggression.

Davidson and colleagues (2003) found that mindfulness could reduce stress and improve immune function after only eight weeks. It also found that mindfulness decreased activity in the parts of the brain associated with negative emotion and increased activity in the parts of the brain associated with positive emotion.

In a comprehensive review of 209 studies, Khoury and colleagues (2013) concluded that mindfulness-based therapy does reduce anxiety, stress and depression.

Greeson (2009) reviewed the results of 52 studies

on mindfulness selected on the basis of their scientific rigour. He concluded that mindfulness induced more positive states of mind, reduced stress hormones, improved immunity and helped people develop more healthy behaviours in terms of eating, sleeping and substance use.

Still not convinced?

Mindfulness has been shown to relieve the pain felt by people with chronic pain and to reduce feelings of depression (Chiesa and Serreti, 2011). This shows what a powerful technique mindfulness can be.

So what evidence is there that mindfulness works on children and teenagers?

One study found that teenagers who had participated in a mindfulness training programme reported feeling more positive than a comparative group of teenagers who had not (Schonert-Reichel and Lawlor, 2010). Wall (2005) taught 11-13 year olds a combination of mindfulness techniques (sitting meditation and mindful eating) and Tai Chi over a five week period. The children reported feeling calmer, less reactive, more relaxed and having better sleep. Another study followed 137 girls at a secondary school following a school-based mindfulness programme over six sessions. They found that the girls showed reductions in self-reported negative feelings, tiredness, aches and pains, and they calmer, more relaxed and improved self-acceptance (Broderick and Metz, 2009).

In addition, research suggests that mindfulness training can improve attention and memory. When students practice mindfulness, they learn to focus, sustain and shift their attention, which has obvious benefits in terms of school work (Napoli et al, 2005; Zylowska et al. 2008).

Gatz and Roemer (2009) found that mindfulness can help students regulate and manage their emotions.

Why is teaching mindfulness in schools so important?

Family issues, peer relationships, learning difficulties and mental health problems can affect the way pupils behave at school. Teaching mindfulness is one way that schools can help create a happy learning environment.

Schools and parents are also increasingly focused on teenagers getting good grades and more and more teenagers are suffering from high levels of anxiety before public examinations. Mindfulness can help teenagers, parents and teachers reflect on what is important as there are many factors that affect success in life such as emotional intelligence not just examinations.

Mindfulness can be used as a preventative measure in schools to protect against mental health issues such as anxiety, depression and self-harming. About 10% of children have a mental health problem at any one time and mindfulness can stop minor problems getting worse. Mindfulness can also make teachers more aware of the individuals in their environment. After all, it is not only students who suffer from mental health issues. A recent survey found that teachers experience some of the highest rates of work-related stress. Practising mindfulness can make teachers more aware of when they need to take a rest and also of their colleagues' needs. Senior leaders in schools who practise mindfulness may begin to see more clearly what elements of their working practices are worth keeping and what can be cut.

So what does a good mindfulness programme for teenagers look like?

A good mindfulness programme will teach teenagers the following:

-To recognise the signs and symptoms of stress.
-To understand the link between their thoughts, feelings and bodily sensations.
-To be able to accept their emotions and thoughts non-judgementally.

-To be able to regulate their emotions.
-To be mindful when carrying out everyday tasks.
-To be mindful when interacting with others.

I have developed a set of twelve sessions that can be used to teach mindfulness. Each session lasts about twenty-five minutes and is better with small groups of students.

Session 1

The first session starts with a questionnaire, which measures perceived stress levels. This can be downloaded for free at www.mindgarden.com. It is important to do this questionnaire at the beginning and the end of the twelve sessions, to see if there have been any changes in the students' perceived levels of stress.

I then give the students a questionnaire to get them to think about what might be causing stress. This includes a list of things that might be causing them stress such as parents, workload, examinations, friends, their appearance etc. and they have to circle the things that are causing them stress. We return to this later.

To introduce the concept of mindfulness and its benefits, I show students the PowerPoint presentation 'Introduction to Mindfulness', which can be downloaded for free from www.fayecarlisle.com. The presentation includes evidence from psychological studies to support mindfulness as the first thing is to convince students that it works. I discuss how mindfulness helps us to focus our attention so that we can control our thoughts and emotions. Students often decide to join the mindfulness sessions because they have had problems in how they deal with other people and they want to deal with their anger better. I explain that mindfulness can help them be less reactive to situations. At this stage, it is important to tell the students that they shouldn't share what people have said during the sessions outside the room as this could make people feel uncomfortable. I also remind them that if something comes up for them in the mindfulness sessions, then they can see a counsellor. If you have a counsellor at your school, I would remind the students where they are based and how to contact them.

After the presentation, I do a sitting meditation with the students. I read the following script:

'Please find a comfortable position on your chair, with your feet on the floor and your hands by your side or on your lap. Your back should be straight but not rigid. Gently close your eyes if you feel comfortable or softly focus on the space in front of you. Now bring your attention to the sensations and movement of breath through your body. Your mind may wander frequently during the meditation. This is normal but you can gently and kindly redirect your attention back to your breathing. Focus on your breath for two minutes

(Pause). Now shift your attention to your bodily sensations. Take note of the contact your body has with the chair or floor and the sensations associated with this. Notice the sensations in your body without judgment, just accept them and reflect on them with curiosity and interest, even if it is unpleasant. Bring awareness to any urges you may have to relieve discomfort, such as moving your body or scratching an itch. Do not act on these urges right away, instead just observe the discomfort with acceptance. If you decide to move then do it mindfully, by observing the intention to move and the change in sensation as a result of moving. You may bring awareness to your environment and listen mindfully to the sounds around you. Notice the volume, tone and duration of the sounds without analysing or judging them. Observe the periods of silence between the sounds also and then redirect your focus to your breathing.

When you notice a thought, observe it briefly without becoming absorbed and then gently return your attention to your breath. If any emotions that come to the surface, just observe the type of emotion you are experiencing such as boredom, excitement or sadness and then redirect your attention to your breath.'

At the end of the meditation, I ask students to reflect on their experiences.

For homework, I encourage the students to do a one minute sitting meditation every day in a quiet place at home, in the car or on the school bus and I reinforce the idea of bringing their attention back to their breath.

Session 2

I generally start the session by asking the student about their experiences of practising the one minute sitting meditation at home.

Usually some of the students will say that they have forgotten to do the meditation. Some will say that they did it a couple of times when they were feeling angry and stressed. So we focus on the experiences of those who have done it.

One session, a student said that she felt really angry about the amount of homework she had to do but after doing the one minute meditation, she calmed down and got on with it. I was surprised (although I didn't say) at how angry the homework had made this student feel but another student agreed that she had felt really angry about homework as well. This has given me an insight as a teacher and allowed me to reflect on how I set my students homework.

I then ask the students who have tried the sitting meditation whether it was difficult or easy for them to concentrate on their breathing during the minute. Many of them will say that before they knew it, their mind had wandered completely onto other things and then the minute was up. You may have students who have carried out the one minute mindfulness exercise every day. Usually they will say that it has helped them feel less stressed. You can ask them whether they have got better at re-focusing their attention on their breath over the period of time.

For those students, who didn't do the meditation, we talk about what might be preventing them from carrying out the mindfulness meditation. They will usually say that although it was only one minute, there often seems to be other things to do such as watching TV or surfing the internet. I encourage them to find just one minute a day to do it by reminding them of the benefits of regular practice of mindfulness. I emphasise the importance of becoming more self-aware and being able to reflect on our thoughts.

I also talk about not adding to negative thoughts. For example, a student who thinks they can't cope with the amount of homework they've got to do might add to that thought by worrying about how they are going to revise for their exams, how they did badly on the last Maths or English test and how they might have to give up their favourite extra-curricular activity. I explain that they can imagine a red stop sign in their head every time they start adding to their negative thoughts.

This discussion is then followed by PowerPoint presentation on the signs of stress and understanding emotions. This PowerPoint 'Stress and Emotions' can be downloaded for free at www.fayecarlisle.com. I follow the presentation by asking the students to think about good and bad stressors in their lives.

We then do a visualisation meditation where students had to imagine being a place that they found relaxing and calming.

I read the following script:

'Begin by sitting in a comfortable position, with your back straight and shoulders relaxed. Softly close your eyes. Allow the picture in your mind to become blank. You are going to imagine a place that feels comfortable, safe, and relaxing. Think of your place. It might be the beach, a lake, or even your own bed. Imagine it slowly appearing before you, becoming more and more clear. Look to your left. What do you see? Look to your right. What is over there? Look closer. Breathe in. What do you smell? Walk around your place. Look closer at certain things. Stay focused on your place. How are you feeling? If you find your thoughts wandering, observe them, and then focus on bringing the image of your place back into focus in front of you. (Allow some time.) When you are ready, put your hand in front of your eyes. Open your eyes. Slowly spread your fingers to allow light in. When you are ready, slowly remove your hand.'

I encourage the students to do a one minute mindfulness meditation every day in the next week and to do the visualisation meditation if they feel stressed or angry.

Session 3

This session focuses on getting students to be more

aware of the present moment. I start by asking them again how they had got on with the one minute mindfulness meditation and whether anyone has tried the visualisation meditation.

I then show them a PowerPoint presentation called 'Living in the Present', which is free to download at www.fayecarlisle.com. The presentation asks them to consider whether they really notice their surroundings or whether they walk around so preoccupied with their own thoughts that they are unaware of the present. We discuss using our senses to really enjoy the present moment. I follow this by talking about mindful eating. Each student is given a large wrapped chocolate of their choice. I talked about how it is easy if we like chocolate a lot to eat it so quickly that we hardly taste it. I read the following script to the students:

'In this exercise, I am going to ask you to take three separate bites of a chocolate. Unwrap the chocolate you have chosen and look at it carefully. Feel the texture of the chocolate between your fingers and notice its colours. Be aware of any thoughts you might be having about the chocolate. Lift the chocolate to your nose and smell it for a while. Now bring the chocolate to your lips. Notice whether your mouth waters at the thought of eating the chocolate. Take one bite of the chocolate and bring it to one side of your mouth. Notice what it tastes like. Now bring the chocolate to the other side of your mouth, slowly experiencing the actual taste of the chocolate. Hold it in your mouth for a second and be aware of whether it is melting. You may now want to start chewing your chocolate. Be aware of the impulse to swallow as it comes up, so that even that is experienced consciously. When you are ready, take a second bite of your chocolate and repeat this process. Please try it again with your final, third bite.'

Often the students will say that eating chocolate slowly in this way helps them to notice the different flavours. They will notice whether you bought them cheap or expensive chocolate!

At the end of the meditation, we talk about whether they are slow or fast eaters and whether they tend to do other things at the same time as eating. I suggest to them that for one meal that week, they eat the end part of their meal mindfully, savouring the taste of the food.

I give the students a list of five mindfulness activities to practise being in the present at the end of the session.

Walk around the school, paying attention your surroundings. Looks at the brickwork, windows, roof etc. Look at the playground. See whether you notice anything you haven't noticed before.
Go for a walk at the park. Look at the trees, plants and flowers. Pay attention to any smells and sounds in your environment.
Listen to some music mindfully. Pay attention to the notes or words in the music that you like.
Get ready for bed slowly. Pay attention to brushing your teeth, putting your pyjamas on and the feel of

the covers as you lie down.
Have a conversation with a friend and really listen
to them without interrupting or checking your
phone.

Session 4

This session I try and arrange to use the school
gym so that the students have more space. If this is
not possible for you, then move the desks back in
your classroom to make space. I provide a yoga
mat for each student.

As usual, I start the lesson by talking to the
students about how they are getting on with the
one minute mindfulness. By the fourth session,
most of the students will be practicing mindfulness
a few times a week if not every day. I then ask
them whether they have done any mindful eating
in the last week. A few students may say that have
done it and then you can ask about their
experiences. You can then ask the other students if
they have done any activities to practise living in
the present. The most popular activity is the one
where they have to listen to music without doing
anything else and really listen for the instruments,
notes or words. They also like the paying attention
to getting into bed at the end of the day. We
discuss whether they have noticed new things
around the school. Sometimes they will be able to

give you detailed information about what they had seen. I encourage them to continue to be mindful in more activities next week.

I then get the students to lie down on their yoga mats to do a body scan meditation. I read them the following script:

'Lie down and find a comfortable position. Gently close your eyes or focus them softly. Now put your arms by your side. Notice the contact your body has with the floor. As I go through the body scan, I'm going to ask you to focus on different parts of your body. Notice how each part feels as we move along. If you feel uncomfortable, you can move but notice the intention to move that part of your body before you do it. First of all, I'd like you to focus on the tips of your toes. What do they feel like? If you can't feel anything just notice that. Now move your attention to bottom of your feet, what do they feel like? Your heel? The tops of your feet? Pause. Now focus on your ankles, what do they feel like? Gradually, move your attention to your calves and then your shins. Notice any contact they have with the floor. Now move your attention to your knees, the backs of your knees and then your thighs. What do they feel like? Now focus on your pelvic area and your posterior. Your back and your shoulders. Notice any tension in your back and shoulders. Pause. Now pay attention to your stomach and your chest. Notice how your stomach and chest rises and fall as you breathe in and out. Pause. Gradually move your attention to your neck and then your face. Notice your cheeks, chin, lips, nose, eyes. Move your attention to your ears. How do they feel? If you can't feel anything, just notice this. Now focus on your forehead, the top of your head and the back of your head. Finally, bring your whole body into focus. How does your whole body feel? Pause. When you're ready, I'd like you to slowly open your eyes if they were closed and bring your attention back to the room.'

At the end of the body scan, I ask the students in turn what their experiences were and whether they liked it or not.

For homework I give the students a sheet with helpful and unhelpful ways of coping with stress. Helpful ways of dealing with stress include taking more exercise, listening to a favourite song, squeezing a stress ball and talking to a friend. Unhelpful ways of dealing with stress include drinking too much alcohol, getting into a fight and isolating yourself. I ask the students to think about the ways they cope with stress for the next session.

Session 5

I start the session with a sitting meditation. I tell them to place their feet on the floor, with their hands either on their laps or at their side in a comfortable but alert position. The theme for the lesson is intention. I discuss with them that the word intention may have negative connotations because we often use the word to mean when we have intended to do something but not managed to do it. For example, we might have intended to read a certain book over the holidays but not managed to finish it or even start it. However, I explain that we will be thinking about our intentions in a more positive way.

I then ask them to place their hands on their belly so that they can feel the rise and fall of their belly as they breathe in and out and how the diaphragm moves up on the in-breath and down on the out-breath.

After the students had been doing the breathing exercise for 5 minutes, I ask them to visualise a clear, still pool of water in their minds and I read the following script:

'In a minute, I am going to ask you to drop a stone into your clear still pool and as you do it I want you to ask yourselves what was your intention in coming to the mindfulness sessions. Okay, now I want you to imagine dropping that stone into your clear still pool and I want you to ask yourself what was your intention in coming to the mindfulness sessions as you watch the ripples form in your pool (Pause). I am now going to ask you to drop a bigger stone into your clear still pool and as it falls deeper into your pool, ask yourself again what was your intention in coming to the mindfulness sessions. Maybe other reasons may come to the surface as you think deeper. Watch and observe your thoughts (Pause). Now just because three is a good number, I am going to ask you to drop one more stone into your deep still pool and now ask yourself again, what was your intention in coming to the mindfulness sessions (Pause). I am now going to ask you to return your attention to your breath. Let any thoughts you had go and focus on your breath. Breathing in one, breathing out one, breathing in two, breathing out two, breathing in three, breathing out three. Keep focusing on your breath now. If your thoughts stray away from your breath, gently bring your thoughts back to your breath (Pause). Now open your eyes slowly. Allow your eyes to re-focus slowly and notice the colours in the room become clearer.'

I then ask each student about their intentions in coming to the mindfulness sessions. When I've done this before, some of the students have said that they wanted a time in the week where they could relax. Other students have talked about wanting to be less stressed and less overwhelmed by their workload. We talk about how mindfulness helps us to shift our attention so that rather than worrying about the 101 things we need to do, we can get on with the most immediate task.

Finally, I return to the homework from last lesson, which was reflecting on how they cope with stress. I ask each student to talk about the helpful ways they use to deal with stress. Students often say that they like listening to music. When they do this, I talk about really listening to the music and trying to pick out certain instruments within the piece. I also discuss how some adults and teenagers might use alcohol as a way of dealing with stress but that it is not particularly helpful. As a contrast, I talk about how regular exercise, for example, going for a run or a walk in the open air can be a helpful way to deal with stress. I had one student tell me that not achieving certain goals during exercise made her stressed. I said to her it is good to stretch ourselves during exercise so that we meet personal goals but it is not a good idea to compare ourselves to others. I talk about noticing and accepting our emotions then letting them go.

As they leave, I encourage the students to keep practising mindfulness at home.

Session 6:

This session, I do a sitting body scan meditation as this is easier in a school classroom. I read the following script:

'Please find a comfortable seated position, with both feet on the floor and your arms at your side or on your lap. Begin by bringing your attention into your body.
Now close your eyes if that's comfortable for you or softly focus your eyes in front of you.
Begin by bringing your attention into your body. Notice the weight of your body on the chair and what it feels like. If you feel uncomfortable, notice this and slowly, mindfully shift your position
Take a few deep breaths.

And as you take a deep breath, bring in more oxygen into your body. And as you exhale, have a sense of relaxing more deeply.

You can notice your feet on the floor, notice the sensations of your feet touching the floor. The weight and pressure, vibration, heat.

Now bring your attention to your left foot. What do your toes on your left foot feel like? You might not being able to feel them, if this is the case just notice that. Now bring your attention to the bottom of your foot. The ball of your foot and now your heel. Gradually shift your attention to the top of your foot, what does that feel like. Now move to your ankle (Pause). Your shin and calf (Pause). What does you left knee feel like? (Pause). Now move your attention to your left thigh. Notice any contact your thigh has with the chair you're sitting on. (Pause). Now notice your left hip and your pelvic area. Now we are going to do the same thing on with your right side. Bring your attention your right foot. What do your toes on your right foot feel like? (Pause) The bottom of your right foot . The ball of your foot and now your heel. Gradually shift your attention to the top of your right foot. What does that feel like? Now move to your ankle (Pause). Your shin and calf (Pause). What does you right knee feel like? (Pause). Now move your attention to your thigh. Notice any contact your thigh has with the chair you're sitting on (Pause). You may notice your legs against the chair. What pressure do you notice? Is there heaviness, lightness, pulsing? (Pause). Now bring your attention up to your hips and then your stomach area. What does your stomach feel like? Try and relax and notice how your stomach rises and falls as you breathe in and out. Bring your attention up your body to your chest. What do you notice as your breathe? Notice your left hand. What do your fingers feel like? The palm of your hand (Pause). The top of your hand (Pause). Now bring your attention to your left wrist (Pause). Your bottom of your left arm, your elbow, your upper arm (Pause). Now we will move to your right side. What your right hand feel like? Your fingers. The palm of your right hand. The top of your hand (Pause). Your wrist. The bottom of your right arm. Your elbow and your upper arm. (Pause). Now notice your shoulders. Is there any tension there? Let your shoulders relax. Notice your neck and throat. Now gradually move your attention to your jaw. Relax your jaw. Let your face and facial muscles relax. What does your chin feel like? Your cheeks. Your nose. Your ears (Pause). Sometimes you may not feel anything, if this is the case, just notice this. Now focus on how your lips feel. Your eyes. Your eyebrows. Your forehead and the top of your head. Now notice your whole body. What does it feel like? Take a few breaths and when you are ready, open your eyes if they are closed and slowly bring your attention back to the room.'

The sitting body scan meditation lasts for about fifteen minutes. After the meditation, I ask the students how they found it. Sometimes they say that they've almost gone to sleep. We talk about trying to sit in an upright and alert position to stay awake as the aim of the meditation is to pay attention to how our body feels. However, I also tell them that they should be mindful of their tiredness. I ask them to consider whether their desire to sleep relates to tiredness or whether it was to do with the mind relaxing and wanting to switch off.

Some students may say they prefer the breathing meditations to the body scan meditation. It can be hard for students to focus their attention on certain parts of the body and they may say that sometimes they couldn't feel anything. For example, when they are asked to focus their attention on their toes, they may say they can't feel their toes. We talk about learning to control our attention and that sometimes our mind may resist focusing on a certain part of the body. We may say to ourselves we are bored with the activity and that there are more interesting things to think about. Then I point out that if we can learn to control where we place our attention, then we are exercising the part of the brain involved in regulation of our attention and emotions. By doing the body scan meditation, we are learning to control are reactivity to situations, our emotions and what we want to focus on.

I then discuss the possibility of the students doing ten minutes of mindfulness a day. Often the students say that they don't think they can give themselves the time for that. We talk about distractions such as TV, internet and texting and I suggest that they should aim to do at least 2 minutes every day. Sometimes the students find it is easier to practise mindfulness just before bedtime but this can lead to them just falling asleep.

Session 7

I start the session with a five minute sitting meditation.

At this stage, I like to introduce a discussion about happiness. We talk about what happiness means to them. Some of the students will say that being with their family, hanging out with friends, playing sport and singing makes them happy. I had one student tell me that she used to love singing when she was younger but stopped when it became more serious. It is important for a teacher of mindfulness not to jump to any conclusions about what someone means so I asked her to elaborate on what she meant. She explained that as she got older, singing became more about performing for others and doing it well rather than just for fun. I said that if singing made her happy, then maybe she could do it in a non-stressful situation such as singing in the shower.

I encourage all the students to do more of the things that make them happy and to give themselves time to do them. I then do a meditation about not feeling guilty about taking the time to do things they enjoy. I read the following script:

'Please find a comfortable seated position, with both feet on the floor and your arms at your side or on your lap. Now close your eyes if that's comfortable for you or softly focus your eyes in front of you. By choosing to do this meditation, you are doing a healthy and productive activity. By practising mindfulness and doing other things that make you happy you can reduce stress and become more efficient. Take a few moments to just breathe. Notice the rise and fall of your stomach as you breathe in and out. Some thoughts might come into your mind of things you need to do. Notice these preoccupations and then let them go. You can return to them later. Redirect your attention to your breathing. If more thoughts come into your head, observe them, then let them pass. Return your attention to your breathing for one minute (Pause). Now I want you to reflect on any thoughts you've had about tasks that you need to do. Notice any judgements or criticisms you've made to yourself. Remember that no one needs to be productive all the time. Take time to just being still for one more minute. Take a deep breath in and as you exhale allow your body to relax. Breathe slowly and calmly. (Pause for one minute). It is okay to relax. It is okay to take the time to do things that make you happy. Now make a note of any intentions you have for the future. And when you are ready, slowly open your eyes if they are closed and bring your attention back to the room.'

At the end of the meditation, I ask the students how they found it and what their intentions are for the future.

For homework, I ask the students to keep a diary of one positive thing they experience each day over the next week. I point out that during any day we might have positive and negative things happen to us and that the way we see a day should not be clouded by one negative situation. I give the students some scenarios to consider. For example, a girl may have got up in the morning in a fairly good mood and had a conversation with her mother about going shopping at the weekend. She then goes to school and during tutor time has an argument with her friend and is put into detention by her teacher for late homework. However, when she gets home, she watches her favourite programme on TV and has a nice dinner with her family. Her day hasn't been all bad but it is possible that she might view it that way if she doesn't manage her thoughts.

Session 8:

This session I talk to the students about stopping unhelpful urges. We discuss anything the students might want to stop doing and then I read the following script:

'Please find a comfortable seated position, with both feet on the floor and your arms at your side or on your lap. Begin by bringing your attention into your body.

Now close your eyes if that's comfortable for you or softly focus your eyes in front of you. Now take a few moments to notice where you experience urges in your body. For example, when you are hungry, you might notice urges in your mouth or in your stomach. Think back to last time you had the urge to do something you want to stop. What part of your body is related to this urge? How does your body react? If the urge is too strong, you may want to pick a different situation, where the urge is less strong. When you have noticed what parts of your body are related to the urge, focus your attention on them. Notice any sensations you feel. Does it feel hot, cold, uncomfortable? What colour might you associate with the urge?

Now bring your attention to your breath. Notice how your stomach rises and falls as you breathe in and out. Do this for 2 minutes. Now gradually shift your attention back to the parts of your body where you noticed the urge. What do you feel now? Is there a difference between how it felt before and after you practised the breathing meditation? As you pay attention to the parts of your body associated with the urge, is there a change in how it feels? Imagine that you are riding a wave of sensations and feelings. Notice these sensations for 1 minute. When you have finished, ask yourself whether the urge feels different. You may want to spend a little time thinking of any intentions you have (Pause). Now open your eyes if they are closed and slowly bring your attention back to the room.'

After the meditation, we talk about how they found it and whether they found it useful. I ask them whether they want to share any intentions they have for the future.

We then discuss the diary that the students were asked to write about their positive experiences. Often students will say they haven't done it. In this instance, I ask them to think carefully about any positive, peaceful or comforting moments in their day so far and write these down. For example, they might have read a good book or eaten a delicious chocolate bar or listened to a really good piece of music. I encourage the students, who have written stuff down, to talk about their experiences. Then I ask them to try writing down their positive experiences again over the next week.

In the last past of the session, I talk to them about mindful stopping. I explain that sometimes we might go over and over a conversation or problem in our head so many times that we don't gain anything from it. Sometimes we need to let go of certain emotions or worries. I ask them to think of something they want to stop worrying about and then I read them the following script:

'Please find a comfortable seated position, with both feet on the floor and your arms at your side or on your lap. Now close your eyes if that's comfortable for you or softly focus your eyes in front of you. I want you to imagine you are walking down a street and I want you to think about the thing you are worrying about. Now imagine a big street sign with the word 'Stop' on it. This big sign is telling you stop thinking about this problem any longer and to let it go. You don't need to worry about it anymore. Now continue walking down this street. If the thought comes back into your mind, imagine the big stop sign in your head again and let the problem go. You feel lighter and more relaxed as you walk down the street. When you are ready open your eyes if they are closed and slowly bring your attention back to the room.'

After we've done this meditation, I talk to the students about whether they might find this an effective technique to stop them ruminating on problems.

Session 9:

At the beginning of this session, I explain to them that we are going to do a five minute breathing meditation. I tell them that I will help them initially to count their breaths up to five and then I will start back at one again. This is a technique to help them focus their attention on their breathing and to stop their mind wandering. They can then continue with the counting in their head if they want to. I read the following script:

'Please find a comfortable seated position, with your feet on the floor and your hands by your side or on your lap. Close your eyes if you feel comfortable or softly focus your eyes in front of you. Now notice the movement of breath through your body. Notice how your stomach rises on your in-breath and falls on your out-breath. You may way want to put your hands on your stomach to feel it. Your mind may wander frequently during the mindfulness meditation. This is normal, just kindly redirect your attention back to your breathing. Sometimes counting five in-breaths and five out-breaths can help you focus on your breathing. So to start you off I will help you count your breaths. Breathing in one, breathing out one, breathing in two, breathing out two, breathing in three, breathing out three, breathing in four, breathing out four, breathing in five, breathing out five. Breathing in one, breathing out one, breathing in two, breathing out two, breathing in three, breathing out three, breathing in four, breathing out four, breathing in five, breathing out five. Now focus on your breathing silently for a few more minutes (Pause for 3 minutes). When you are ready open your eyes if they were closed and gradually bring your awareness back to room.'

We then talk about any positive experiences they have experienced in the last week. I ask them to discuss any body sensations and feelings they can identify related to their positive experiences. In one session, a student told me that she hadn't had any positive experiences in the last week because she'd been ill. I asked her whether she had had any nice food when she'd been ill or read any good books and then she remembered that her mother had bought her some nice magazines to read. In this session, I remind the students that life is made up of positive moments, which we should try to enjoy and negative moments that we can learn will pass.

The second part of the session involves getting students to understand the link between their thoughts and emotions. I ask the students to close their eyes and imagine the following situation: 'You are walking down a street and you see someone on the other side of the street. You wave at them but they don't wave back and they continue walking on.' What are your thoughts? How do you feel? What body sensations are there?

Once the students have opened their eyes, we talk about what they had visualised and how this had made them feel. Students often say that it made them feel angry at being ignored. I explain how it is good to recognise how our thoughts and emotions are linked. I then show them a Powerpoint on how our thoughts and emotions are connected. This can be downloaded at www.fayecarlisle.com. I talk about recognising our emotions about certain events. Mindfulness is not about getting rid of our emotions but about being aware of them. There is a misunderstanding that we should not have strong negative emotions but in mindfulness, we learn to recognise that these are part of life but that we don't have to be overwhelmed by them.

At the end of the session I ask students to keep a

diary of any negative moments they have in the next week and any feelings and body sensations they have at the time. I tell them that they can write it down at the end of the day and notice any changes in perspective or feelings since the incident.

Session 10

I start this session with the same five minute breathing meditation from session nine.

We then do a movement practice in a sitting position. I read the following script to them:

'We are now going to try a movement practice. Please find a comfortable position on your chair with both feet on the floor and your arms at your side or on your lap. First of all I would like you to flex your right foot up and curl your toes under. Notice the feeling of your heel on the floor, the upper part of your foot, your ankle and your toes. Now flex your right foot up and down three times. See whether you can tell the difference between the feeling of your right and left foot on the floor. We are now going to repeat the process with your left foot. Flex your left foot up and curl your toes under. Notice the feeling of your heel on the floor, the upper part of your foot, your ankle and your toes. Now flex your left foot up and down three times. What do both feet feel like now? (Pause). I am now going to ask you to close your eyes and move the top of your head gently to the left side. Now move your neck and finally move from your waist sideways. When you are ready come up by first moving your waist, then your neck and finally your head. I would like you to do this three times on your left hand side (Pause while they do it). Notice the difference in the movement of the head, neck and waist. When you have finished doing the left side, I want you to repeat the process on the right side of the body with the head, neck and waist movements being done separately. Move the top of your head gently to the right side. Now move your neck and finally move from your waist sideways to the right. When you are ready come up by first moving your waist, then your neck and finally your head. Now do this three times on your right hand side (Pause while they do it). Notice how both sides of your body feel (Pause). When you are ready gently open your eyes and come back to the room.'

After the movement practice, we discuss how they found it. Then we talk about any negative moments they have had in the last week. In one class, I had a student tell me that she didn't really like remembering negative moments and she felt it wasn't a good thing to do. I told her that I could see why she didn't want to remember negative moments but as we can't stop them, we can learn to deal with them better using mindfulness techniques.

Next I explain the three minute breathing space. The first minute of the meditation involves becoming aware of where we are right now and any thoughts and feeling we might have. The second minute of the meditation involves focusing on our breath and letting any thoughts and feeling go. The third minute of the meditation involves expanding awareness again to take in firstly body sensations, and then any thoughts and feelings. I explain that it can be useful to notice and be curious about any differences in perspective they have after the three minute breathing space.

I read the following script:

'Please find a comfortable seated position, with both feet on the floor and your arms at your side or on your lap. Close your eyes if you feel comfortable or gently focus on the space in front of you. I want you to become aware of where you are right now and any thoughts and feelings you might have (Pause for one minute). Now I want you to focus on your breathing and let any thoughts or feelings go (Pause for one minute). In this final minute, I want you to expand your awareness. Notice any sensations in your body (Pause). Now notice any thoughts and feelings you have (Pause). Are there any differences in perspective? (Pause). When you are ready, open your eyes if they were closed and slowly come back to the room.'

After doing this exercise, I ask for feedback from the students. One student told me that she had been thinking about a girl who had been annoying her before the exercise but after focusing on her breathing during the three minute breathing space, it didn't seem as important. Another student told me that she thought it gave her perspective in the way she was thinking about a difficult situation at home.

Session 11

This session starts with a five minute sitting meditation. We then talk about mindful stopping and the three minute breathing space to see whether any of them have used the techniques recently. Some students might say that they have used it in at difficult moments when they were getting annoyed or angry.

I then do a walking meditation around the school for fifteen minutes. Before, we set off I tell them not to talk to each other as although this is a temptation, we are trying to really focus on what it feels like to walk and take in our surroundings. When we start the walk, I ask them to notice the pressure of their heels on the floor and the ball of their foot as they lift their feet and place their feet down again. I ask them to feel the weight shift onto each foot as their body moves forward. At first we walk slowly and then I ask the students to walk faster to see if they can notice any difference. I ask them to observe the movements of their hands and arms and to notice how their head feels balanced on their neck and shoulders. I then ask them to notice their breathing. After five minutes of doing this, I suggest that they pay attention to the sounds around them. I also ask them to use their eyes to really take in their surroundings as there may be aspects of their surrounding that they have previously taken for granted. This could be the brickwork of the buildings or any trees around the school.

At the end of the walking meditation, we discuss their experiences. Often students will say that it was difficult to focus because of other students around the school. However, they usually say they enjoyed it too. I talk to them about doing the walking meditation in their daily life. For example, when they are walking to school or to the shops. I explain to them that they can use these moments to really focus on being in the present rather than replaying conversations or worrying about the future. I also point out that they can bring the same degree of awareness to every activity they do whether it be having a shower or getting dressed or eating.

Session 12

For the last session in the programme, I tell students that we will be looking at dealing with difficulties in our lives. I start with a five minute breathing meditation.

Then I read them a poem called 'The Guest House':

This being human is a guest house.
Every morning a new arrival.

A joy, a depression, a meanness,
some momentary awareness comes
as an unexpected visitor.

Welcome and entertain them all!
Even if they are a crowd of sorrows,
who violently sweep your house
empty of its furniture,
still, treat each guest honorably.
He may be clearing you out
for some new delight.

The dark thought, the shame, the malice.
meet them at the door laughing and invite them in.

Be grateful for whatever comes.
because each has been sent
as a guide from beyond.

> Jellaludin Rumi,
> translation by Coleman Barks

I ask them to note any feelings or thoughts they
have about the poem. We then discuss the poem
together. I explain that the purpose of mindfulness
is not to create positive thinking but to become
more aware of our thoughts and emotions. It is
about recognising that life will have both suffering
and joy and to understand that these moments will

pass. If we can observe our thoughts from a certain distance, then we will find it easier to cope with whatever life brings us. This is emotional resilience.

At the end of this final session, I ask students to complete the stress questionnaire again and we discuss how they feel. I encourage them to continue practising mindfulness at home. I use the questionnaires to assess whether there is any reported difference in the stress levels of the students.

How to avoid pitfalls

Sometimes students may feel self-conscious about taking part in a meditation. I experienced this when I had a group of all girls and then suddenly a group of boys joined the group. At first the students couldn't help giggling and they were not able to concentrate very easily on the meditation. Even if one or two students are giggling, it can be difficult for the other students to focus. There are a number of ways you can deal with this scenario. One way is to get the students to all stand up and take a walk around the room. Moving can distract students from their original train of thought. After you have taken a walk round the room, you might say that you will try a different meditation with them. Say that the other one wasn't working and that this other one might work. Tell the students that if they feel they can't concentrate still that they can leave the room quietly and come back in when they are ready.

You can also ask the students to turn their chairs so they are facing a wall or in a direction where they can't see each other. This can eliminate distractions.

I have done a body scan meditation before, where all the students started giggling. I was worried that the students weren't getting much out of the activity but afterwards, they said they had really liked it despite the giggling. They also said could they do another meditation before they had to go. This time, I decided to do a walking meditation, which the students did not giggle during.

Should mindfulness sessions be compulsory or optional?

Mindfulness works better with a group of students who have opted to take part. If the students have chosen to come to the mindfulness sessions, they are more likely to take it seriously and feel that they have something to learn.

So what do you do if you have a group of students who have not chosen to take part?

A group of students who have been forced to take part in a mindfulness session may not be so receptive. Some students may feel that it is a waste of time. When a teacher has to work with students who don't want to be there, more time needs to be spent on convincing them of the usefulness of mindfulness before starting on the activities. You may want to spend more time on body scan meditations, which focus their thoughts on certain parts of the body rather than silent meditations.

What happens if issues arrive during a mindfulness session?

Make sure you have a counsellor in place. Provide contact details for your school's counsellor in the first session and remind them of where they can seek help regularly. Practising mindfulness can make students more aware of their emotions and these may need to be dealt with by a counsellor.

Should mindfulness sessions be single sex?

I have done both mixed- and single-sex sessions. Both can work equally well. However, when I have had single-sex groups, they have been more willing to talk about their anxieties about relationships and appearance. Teenagers may feel more comfortable speaking about their concerns in a single-sex environment.

The Teenage Brain

Students may find it useful to understand more about their brains. Previously, people thought that the teenage brain was much like an adult brain and that the really important brain development occurred in the early years. However, neuroscientists have found that teenage brains are still developing. The brain rewires during the teen years and this can continue until the early twenties. New connections between nerve cells in the brain are formed and some connections are lost. The part of the brain that is most affected is the prefrontal cortex, which is important for controlling emotions, empathy and decision-making. The prefrontal cortex helps us to plan ahead, control our impulses and understand the consequences of our actions so it is not surprising that teenagers can be reactive and have problems with self-control. Teenagers may not fully appreciate the consequences of their actions and they may not weigh up information in the same way adults do. So although adults might weigh up the full consequences of bunking a lesson, teenagers may not. Research shows that mindfulness increases activity in the prefrontal cortex, which can help teenagers be less impulsive.

Teenagers can also find it difficult to read facial expressions and recognise other people's feelings while the brain is rewiring. One study found that only 50% of teenagers could recognise fear as a facial expression compared to 100% of adults. So teenagers need help recognising other people's feelings. Mindfulness helps teenagers to become more aware of their own thoughts and feelings but it can also help them become more aware of others too.

Self-Control

Developing teenager's self-esteem is important but it is not the key to happiness that psychologists originally thought. Self-control appears to be the really important element in happiness and it refers to the ability to control our thoughts and emotions. In the late 1960s, Walter Mischel, a professor at Stanford University in the USA, started looking at self-control in young children. The children were given a marshmallow and were told that they could either eat the marshmallow straight away or if they were willing to wait 15 minutes, they could have two marshmallows. Some children were able to wait but others could not. Many years later, Mischel, sent a questionnaire to the children's parents and teachers. He wanted to find out if there was a relationship between the children's self-control at 4-years- old and their ability deal with problems, get along with peers and perform well at school. Mischel found that the children, who had been able to delay gratification so that they received two treats, scored higher on S.A.T tests and had fewer behaviour problems at school. They also found it easier to get along with their peers compared to the children who had less self-control and ate their treat straight away.

Other studies show that self-control is a far better predictor of academic performance than I.Q. Wright et al. (1999), followed individuals from birth to 21 years old and found that those with lower self-control scores in childhood were more likely to be involved in crime although good relationships with parents helped mediate against this. People with poor self-control may not be able to control their impulses. They may lash out at someone in a fight or they may tempted by others into criminal behaviour.

Self-control is the key to success in life at work and in relationships and it can be taught. If we have self-control at work, we won't lose our temper when our boss reprimands us and if we have self-control in relationships, we won't say something we later regret to our partner. Studies show that self-control is a far better predictor of academic performance than IQ. Teenagers with self-control are better able to stop themselves watching TV or texting their friends when they should be revising for exams so they are more likely to do well in exams. So IQ is not the most important factor in performance.

Self-control impacts on physical health and mental well being. Many of us may have experienced setting ourselves certain goals or resolutions, only to give up on them after a few weeks. At New Year, you might have planned to cut down on chocolate and other treats but given in as soon as you've seen a delicious piece of chocolate cake. However, if we develop our self-control we can prevent ourselves having another piece of chocolate cake. Although I have to admit I am not so good at this. What I am a bit better at is doing exercise. If we have self-control, we can push ourselves to go to the gym or go for a run even when we don't feel like it. I often feel a real sense of wellbeing after I've gone for a run and I try to savour this feeling as it keeps me motivated. Self-control also affects mental wellbeing. If we have self-control, we can stop ourselves worrying and ruminating about a conversation we've had with our boss so we are less likely to suffer stress and anxiety. We can also prevent ourselves adding to certain thoughts. For example, we may worry that an acquaintance doesn't like us, and then we may add to this by thinking of instances where we haven't gelled with other people. Once people start on a negative train of thought, they can find it difficult to stop themselves.

So how can teachers develop their students' self-control?

-Improve their understanding of their own and other people's emotions.
-Help them to control their thought and emotions.
-Teach them skills of reflection and taking different perspectives.

Mindfulness can improve self-control as it involves paying attention to the present moment and becoming more aware of thoughts and feelings. It also involves being able to let go of thoughts and feelings that cause us anxiety.

I often ask students whether they spend too much time worrying about a conversation they've had with a friend or whether they spend too much time worrying about how they are going to revise for their exams. I explain that the people who experience the least stress at school are often the people who just focus on completing one task at a time. This allows us to find peace and enjoyment in the present moment.

One student who attended my mindfulness sessions argued that if you stop yourself thinking about problems in the future it just delays the problems for later. I asked her whether if she could find peace in just one minute a day then wasn't that a good thing?

Thoughts, Emotions and Stress

It is important to explain to students that sometimes people's thoughts can be wrong. Use scenarios with your students to demonstrate alternative ways of thinking.

Example 1: A boy may think that he can do nothing about a bully at school? What could he do?

Example 2: A girl from school is walking on the other side of the street, you wave at her but she doesn't wave back. What do you think about her? Are there alternative explanations for her behaviour?

Example 3: Your friends meet up without you. What do you think? Are there alternative explanations?

Example 4: You get rejected from a job. What do you think? Are there alternative explanations?

Emotional intelligence (EI) refers to the ability to express and control our own emotions and to understand, interpret, and respond to the emotions of others. Dulewicz and Higgs (1999) found that people high in emotional intelligence were more likely to do well in the workplace. Mayer and Salovey (1997) showed that people high in emotional intelligence are better able to adapt to different social situations. High scores on emotional intelligence tests are better at predicting leadership potential in the workplace and happiness in romantic relationships that people's scores on traditional IQ tests.

Teenagers need to be able to recognise their own feelings before they can control them. As part of a mindfulness programme, students can be taught different words for expressing their emotions. For example, you might ask them for different words to describe feeling happy, sad, anxious or excited. How many words can you think of for anxiety? The following words can be used to explain feeling anxious: Worried, afraid, threatened, cautious, hesitant, distrustful, embarrassed, freaked out and uneasy. Developing a teenager's emotional vocabulary will help them identify their own feelings better.

Teenagers can also be taught to recognise certain facial expressions. A free PowerPoint called 'Stress and Emotions' can be downloaded from www.fayecarlisle.com with a quiz on recognising emotional expressions.

Students need to understand that pressure and stress aren't always bad for us. Too much pressure can result in us feeling overwhelmed. Too little pressure can make us feel demotivated. Stress is the body's way of rising to a challenge and getting ready to deal with a difficult situation. We need a bit of stress so that we can perform at our best in an exam or in a sport's match. However, prolonged stress can be bad for us and lead to mental health problems.

Signs of prolonged stress include feeling worried, sick, dizzy, and tired and feeling you can't cope even when there is no immediate threat.

There are many strategies to deal with prolonged and unhealthy stress such as getting more sleep, exercising, taking time out to relax and eating healthily. Mindfulness is one technique that can be used to reduce stress.

Case study

At one school I worked at, many students were

experiencing high levels of stress and anxiety around examination time. Some cases were referred to the counsellor but we needed something to help the students with mild stress. As a result, the school introduced a programme to teach students about stress and anxiety. This included explaining the differences between good and bad stress. Mindfulness was one aspect of the programme. Students were taught about mindfulness as part of the PSHE programme for one lesson only but those who wanted to know more were encouraged to attend extra sessions at lunchtime. The set of twelve sessions I delivered started at the beginning of each term.

How often should mindfulness be practised?

It important that people make time for mindfulness on a regular basis as studies show that the more time spent in mindfulness practice, whether at home or in a group, affects how well we deal with stress and how positive our emotions are (Brown et al. 2007; Speca et al. 2000). Therefore, schools are well placed for encouraging mindfulness as a routine part of the day. For example, tutors can encourage their tutees to spend one minute practising mindfulness at morning registration and one minute at afternoon registration. If students start their work feeling calm, they are more likely to be able to concentrate and learn. The one minute break allows students to find their own sense of peace and helps them focus on the most immediate tasks, rather than stressing about everything they have to do or their relationships with other students.

Download Free Mindfulness PowerPoint presentations and teaching resources at www.fayecarlisle.com

.

Printed in Great Britain
by Amazon